Moose Tales

Written by: Carly Tumlinson
Illustrated by: Nelson Tumlinson

Copyright © 2020 Nelson Tumlinson
All rights reserved.

Published by: Tumlinson Homestead
ISBN: 978-0-578-73067-7

Edited by: Julia Allen

For our precious children who make life so much sweeter.

Wyatt Eber Nixon
&
Juliet Emerson Noe

Long ago in a faraway forest, there was a great big moose whose name was Horace.

He was tall and grand
and chocolaty brown
and had antlers on his head
like a beautiful crown.

He had a happy life eating grass and leaves.
He didn't think he could be happier...
And then he met Eves.

Eves was so cute, dainty, and small,
all rolled up in a tiny ball.

Horace was bewildered when he first saw the sight
of something rolling on the ground
in such a hurried fright.

"What could this be?" he asked,
though no one was around.
Then it opened up slowly,
stretching out on the ground.

"How do you do?" asked Horace in a loud, slow bellow. "I'm doing mighty fine," Eves whispered, for she was rather mellow.

"What ARE you?" Horace asked the little creature quite loudly.

"Well," said Eves, "I'm a hedgehog." And she said it rather proudly.

"I'm all alone and looking for home," she said. "I can help!" he replied. "So climb up on my head."

Eves could see for miles from up so high.

She liked the open view; she loved the blue sky.

She wasn't scared on Horace's head.

"Actually," she thought, "it would make a nice bed."

On top of his head,
she curled up in a ball. "Be careful, Eves,"
Horace said. "Please don't fall."

"I won't," she said. "I'm just getting cozy."
"Oh look!" said Horace.
"There's my friend Miss Rosie."

Rosie was such a pretty little fox
who loved to sing and loved to hop.

She leaped right onto Horace's head and sang about how her fur was red.

The three were a silly sight to see.
They became quick friends very easily.

They laughed and sang while
they searched for Eves' house.
On the way, they bumped into
a little grey mouse.

The little mouse was bold and furry.
He introduced himself with a bow,
"My name is Murray."

The three thought Murray was really quite funny,
so they invited him along on their little journey.

All four continued their search once again, enjoying the company of such kind friends.

At last they found Eves' home
and said their goodbyes.
They gave each other hugs
with tears in their eyes.

Though they didn't want to go,
they knew that they should;
so they headed back home
into the big green wood.

Made in the USA
Coppell, TX
28 August 2020